# Bouquet of poems

## Golden words

Gargi Banerjee

BookLeaf Publishing

India | USA | UK

Made with ❤ on the BookLeaf Publishing Platform
www.bookleafpub.in
www.bookleafpub.com

*Bliss*

*The silent night beckons,*

*The sky is lit up with the stars.*

*Oh! The Eternal beauty mesmerises.*

*The hands reach out higher and higher.*

*How far can you go?*

*The sparkling waters*

*Of the river has a story to tell*

*Can you hear the murmur?*

*Is it a tale of misery and sadness?*

*Can you hear the agony?*

*The cries of the world reach you*

*But you are helpless!*

*As helpless as the gazing stars above*

*A hug, a smile, or a gentle touch*

*How long can one wait for that moment of Bliss?*

# Poem 1

A moment of joy.
These days I somehow find myself
Often standing near that window.
The same window from where you first
appeared.
I remember that day, that rain-drenched day.
The world shook with the sound of thunder.
The pavements were wet and slippery
I saw you looking for something.
I was drawn to your face, not a very pretty
one
But a face I have kept alive in my heart.
You were there only for a moment.
Yet you filled that moment with joy
Gloomy rainy day sparkled with light—
The light of Love and warmth.
I embraced it with gratitude.

# Poem 2

A beautiful golden-yellow sand
Red, orange, and yellow rays streaming over
the land,
Where the children run and play.
With the wind blowing where they lay.
Little hands, and little feet,
In the golden light, the breeze is blowing,
gentle and sweet.
There is so much you can feel, the earth's
silent kiss.
There is nothing to fear;
The clouds pass by, wiping away your tears!
Close your eyes and know.
The Universe has a path which it will show!

# Poem 3

A tree-lined road.
Look! Look! The trees are smiling.
As the rain falls, the leaves shudder.
Feeling the drops of water.
They are now reborn again.
The parched Earth,
The ground dry and forlorn;
The despair and misery—
All gone!
Now the leaves can dance with joy.
Look up to the sky.
In ecstasy and gratefulness.

# Poem 4

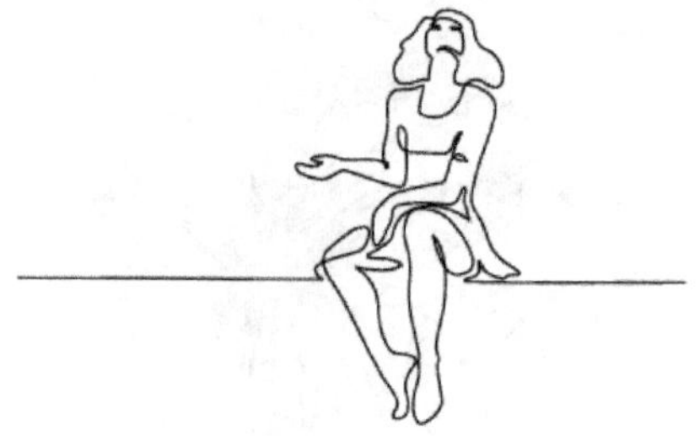

You smile that sweet gentle smile
The eyes, bright and kind.
Once you walked softly on this earth
You - who never stopped your journey.
Day and Night, I felt your soothing touch,
When my forehead burnt
With fever.
Did you not once feel the agony of Life?
The sufferings, the dreams, which just floated
by?
Like clouds, on the distant horizon.
Did you not once feel the pangs—
Of broken desires passing by?
Did your smile hide all that you longed for?
On this day, dear Mother, I bow down to you
You - who now lie in Eternal Slumber!

# Poem 5

Long time ago in a village small
There were beautiful trees, green and tall.
The children played joyfully in the park.
While the birds chirped, the sparrow and the
lark.
The Flowers danced gently in the breeze
The blue sky was a playground for the
graceful geese.
Old ladies sat knitting, while time stood still.
The church bell rang from the faraway hill.
Men passed by with a gentle smile,
Tipped their hats and stood for a while.
The ladies were all a happy lot
Wearing fancy clothes from the village shop
they bought.

Mothers with prams came out for their
evening walk.
Always ready to shake hands and talk.
But alas one day, all the men disappeared,
Went away to towns and cities which they
had feared
Away went the Mothers, babies and all;
No children played with their bat and ball.
The village looked lonely, dark and sad.
No one thinks about all the fun they had.

# Poem 6

The girl stood still, looking at the far distance.
Her long hair tied with a yellow ribbon
Her face looked sad as if waiting for someone.
The sari was the same that she wore that day!
The day she had seen him coming to say
goodbye.
Their eyes had met, hands had touched.
Tears of sorrow, of pain, had fallen in vain.
Why did fate snatch away
Her only happiness?
He walked away, never looking back.
Did the gentle breeze, the Flowers, feel her
sorrow?

She walked home slowly,
Her feet tired and aching
Years have passed, time has moved on;
Days and nights were the same.
But she came to stand for a moment,
The place where they had parted to say
goodbye.

# Poem 7

The majestic river flows through the town;
The muddy waters winding far, far away.
It's a long journey—a journey carrying many
stories
Stories of struggle, joy, stories of pain.
Men have sat, women have cried near her
Shore.
Their pensive thoughts, and despair;
Their hope and loneliness, the river has
carried
With its flow—never-ending and eternal.
She has embraced many untold secrets of
men.
Silently, without once complaining.
Not rejecting all those who came seeking
solace.

# Poem 8

That tree stood strong and beautiful
Its branches spread out, the green leaves,
vibrant and alive.
The little birds looked out to a world
unfamiliar and strange!
The mother knew as she flew far away.
One day soon her little ones will have wings
to fly.
Wings to take them far away from her.
But now she has work to do, her little ones
are hungry.
She is in a hurry to go back to her Nest.
She can hear their cries—
Oh Lord, please keep them with me for some
more time!
Soon she will fly back to an empty Nest.

# Poem 9

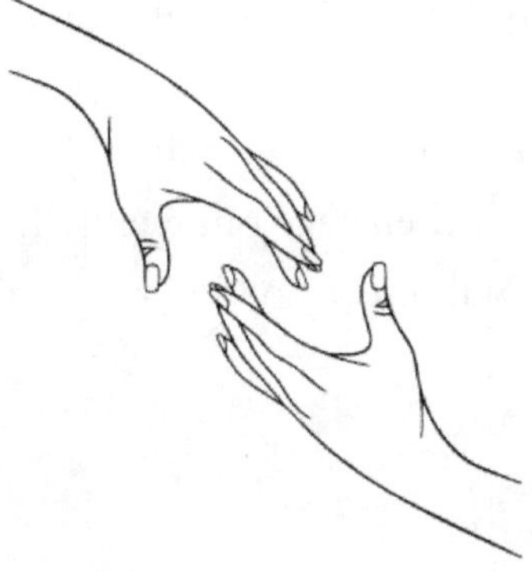

They met after years—
Two friends, they remember their school
days.


Where they talked about their joy and fears;
Oh! how they longed for those days—
Where they went to play in the park,
When they jumped and sang, waking up with
the sun's rays.
The school bell rang, the gates would shut
Walking together they would slowly go to
class.

They envied the gardener, who lived in that
hut,
He spends days with the flowers and trees
Went joyfully to work, all rules he could
flout..
So today they met, their hair white and grey
Wrinkles on their face but eyes still shine,
Now they will meet, to God they will pray!

# Poem 10

She walked alone, her bright skirt swaying
She was humming a tune, her heart joyfully
dancing.
The Flowers bloomed, the sky was clear;
The butterflies pranced; the birds chirping
you could hear.
She was feeling happy today—for no reason at
all.
Her father was coming home, they were
waiting for his call.
He was fighting a battle for so many years
As war raged on, they lived in fear.
But now the war's over, there is peace
everywhere.
Her Father's now a hero; they will have much
love to share.

# Poem 11

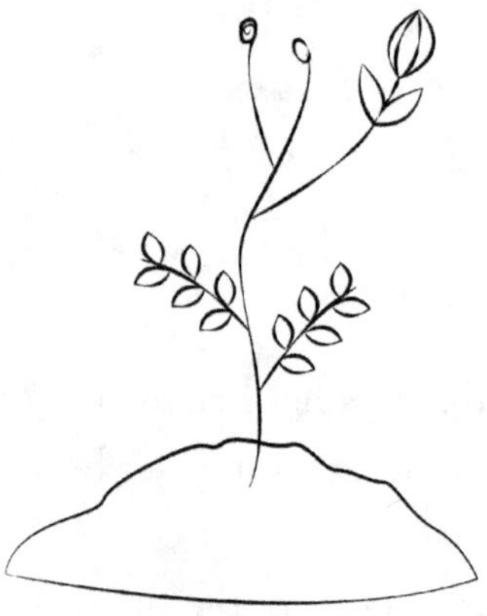

We walked along the forest trail -
The trees stood tall, had their stories to tell.
One little bird sitting there—
Looked sad and solemn, but what do we care?
All through the night the men had come
They brought the machines, one could hear
their hum
The big trees were cut, the branches fell;
No one protested as they created our hell.

Mother Nature saw it all and dropped a
sorrowful tear.
Big cities will be built, so the land was
cleared.
No birds will sing, no flowers bloom;
The trees will die which will add to our
gloom.
Many will say, 'What a sad affair!'
'What can one do?' they will say in despair!!
And life will go on, years will go by,
Who will hear when the trees they will sigh?

# Poem 12

I am free as a bird.
I can fly, far, far away.
Never come back!
The trees are my home!
The sky looks so blue! I am free.
The walls cannot stop me.
The rooms cannot confine me.
I can sweep past the town;
I can dance with the waves.
I can sing with the birds.
I am free, I am free, I am free.
The wild geese are flying
The ducks are swimming by.

The water is blue
I can see everything through.
My soul feels light
There is no one in sight.
Only the waves and the Sea,
The beach and the breeze.
I am free, I am free, I am free.

# Poem 13

The caravan moved along the desert sand.
The hot sun blazed, the air was still.
The camels were bleating as they walked by
The palm trees swayed, their leaves gently
drooping.
The women wearing red and green skirts sang
gaily.
Their bangles jingled as they moved their
hands.
They were all going to the weekly Bazaar.
They laughed and chatted, now they have not
much to do;
The men with turbans dozed and dreamt of
the cool night sky.
Oh! Now they can rest their aching feet.
The camels will sleep peacefully as the sun
will go down
The women too will rest and sing gently to
their babies!
The day is over—now the stars are shining.

# Poem 14

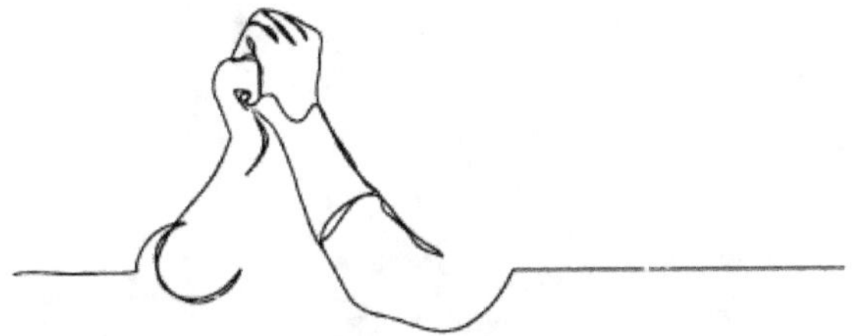

The old man sat in the park
Watching the children play,
Once upon a time, his life was not so dark.
There were children and a happy home—
Now they have gone to far-off lands!
They are young, the world they can roam
Never once moved from the old house near
the Lake.
The house was full of memories, laughter and
fun.
The smell of cakes his wife used to bake.
Slowly years passed by, there is no one left.
His wife left him, only her old coat was there.
Some knitting needles and some photographs
he has kept.

# Poem 15

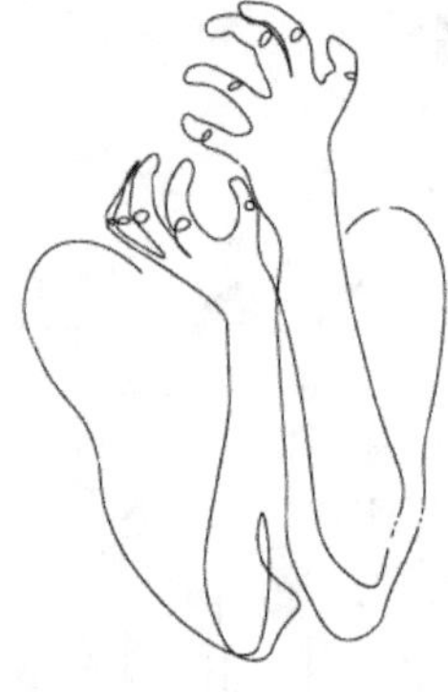

Once there was a girl—
A sweet little girl.
A girl with stars in her eyes,
A girl who wanted to grow up fast.
She wanted to live with dignity.
She wanted to heal men and women.
And so she did.
A doctor she was, with miles to go.
But suddenly - all went dark.

One miserable night they came—
They came to take away her dreams.
They battered and tortured her
They were cowards who butchered her.

Butchered her when she was alone and
sleeping.
As the world slept, she was brutally put to
sleep..
One more helpless girl taken away from us.
A  girl who had stars in her eyes.
A girl who could give us so much.
But she was silenced!
One brave soul lost forever.

# Poem 16

She stood near the waters, watching the ships
go by
That day not so far away, she had been there.
Where the waves had met the sand.
The sky met the faraway horizon
The day was bright with the clouds floating
by.
She had walked slowly to the Sea
Watching the ships sail from faraway land.
She who dreamt of a country where there is
only joy.
Joy and harmony where we all are safe—
Safe from tyranny, safe from cruelty.
The ships can take her there
A new life will begin.
She will leave behind all the sorrow.

She will leave behind all the pain!
A new day, a new life will begin
But the ships never stopped.
Never once saw her standing.
So again, she has come—
She has come for the ship
A ship which will stop for her!

# Poem 17

I have not met him ever.
I have seen his photograph hanging—
Hanging in my mother's bedroom.
A man with kind eyes.
A beautiful smile, and a gentle look.
Alas, he lived not to see his children grow.
Never once could he find the path to take him
home;
A home he had to leave with dreams still
unfulfilled.
Now, he just looks down on you.
Trying to say what is still left unsaid—
Words of love and longing
A man who you miss every moment of your
life.

# Poem 18

It's dawn! The fisherman took his boat out—
Out to the Sea, the day is warm and still.
He looked up and saw some dark clouds.
Oh! Will there be a storm?
But go he must, food must be bought!
The children will be waiting
Waiting with hunger and sorrow!
He could see the sadness in their eyes,
No! He cannot wait any more.
He pushed the boat into the sea,
One last time, he looked up—
Looked up to see the clouds again.
Are they trying to say something?
Are they whispering a warning!
But go he must
The children are waiting!

Suddenly the storm clouds gathered - dark
and dismal
The rain fell without pity
Fell on his little boat!
One last time, he looked up
One last time, he saw their faces,
Then darkness—and all was still.
The relentless waves lashed on the Shore.
Will it bring back the little boat?
Will he come back home again?

# Poem 19

The children are silently passing each day
Quietly crying, crying for justice.
While society waits with anxiety.
Waits for justice which is not there.
Bright young children with dreams
They feel for us, feel for the aged
Fighting against a rotten system
A system perpetrated by a heartless, soulless
society.
We are parents,
Seeing the lives of our children sinking.
Everyday our prayers are with them
God up there, are you listening? Are you
listening to our cries?
Heart beating for them!

They were dragged, pushed
Some of them - their weak bodies
Denied even a drop of water!
STOP them, they are carrying water
STOP them, they are carrying banners!!
Dear children, we need you -
We need you to live.
The lumpens, the unscrupulous, the tyrants,
They surround us
We are losing all that is good.
What will we be left with?

# Poem 20

The drums are beating far away.
You can hear their rhythm
The sound of conch shells.
The Pandals are lit, the lights burning bright.
A small crowd gathers.
The children pulling their mothers.
The young ones are all dressed
Sharing laughter and joy.
But still, somewhere not far,
There are many—
Many who have come with love in their
hearts,
Love for their children
Who are not in the Pandals.

Who are not sharing laughter and joy.
Fathers and mothers who feel for each other!
Waiting for Divine Intervention.
Waiting for Maa to smile and Bless them
When Maa will slay the Demons—
Demons who, with their evil powers,
Have slain a daughter;
Our children are hurting and in pain.

# Poem 21

We are all travellers
One day, we think we are here—
Here where everything is familiar.
The world is ours,
We know where we are going!
Next day the Sun shines again—
But it's different,
Somehow we are all strangers!
We leave our little world,
It's no longer ours!
We move again to an unfamiliar place;
We know the Day ends and Night begins.
Like birds we fly!
The vast expanse of sky is our home.

# Poem 22

Look at the sky!
It's dark but one star shines!
Shines for us, for you and me!
The way is not lost.
Our tears are not in vain.
As we move on, our footsteps slowly follow
A path towards the light!
One lone star is enough,
One ray of hope!
For mankind to rise again!

# Poem 23

The man walked alone, along the highway.
It was dark and raining hard!
Not a soul in sight!
The car lights flashed by;
The lone man was not afraid
The dark night was his companion!
Far away, an owl hooted - calling his mate!
It was not long ago that he had someone—
Someone he could call his friend!
His soulmate, one who was there.
Suddenly the chair was empty
He stood alone and lonely!
Looking up to the sky
His questioning gaze asked the Universe
Why? Why?
Why was there an empty chair!

The Seagulls flew by.
Their white shimmering wings
Looked beautiful.
They answered not!
The vast expanse of the sea
Looked grim and dark!
Why, oh why did they not answer?
The tears rolled by—no one answered!
No one to hold his hand.
No one to embrace him.

# Poem 24

One day comes, merging into night.
I sit still, the sound of machines whirring by.
Early morning, no birds chirp!
The trees have long gone!
The birds have left!
I can see the broken walls and doors.
The windows which once opened
To let in the sun.
Today, only the ruins one can see.
I wake up with a heavy heart!
The long day stretches, unending!
There is no laughter, no one cares
Only the houses stare at you.
You close your eyes - the green grass.
The sea and the sand
All are a distant dream!

# Poem 25

The little Flowers open, they spread their
fragrance.
The bees and the butterflies swarm near them.
The child looks with wonder.
The little creatures go about
Busy as ever.
The child looks at them
His hands move to embrace them
But they cannot see.
They fly away, far, far away.
The child can no longer see
Tears fill up his eyes.
The garden looks empty now!
Darkness descends
It's time to go home!

# Poem 26

The old house stands, majestic and alone!
Years have gone, gone are the laughter of
children.
Gone is the mother's voice calling them,
Calling them to stop their play!
With sorrow in their hearts, they leave their
play.
The big room, the large windows
The High walls are all there
But no children play
No childish chatter echoes
They are all gone
Left to face their destiny.
But the house remains
Strangers lead their lives
Within the High walls,
Within the big rooms.
It now has a new story to tell!

# Poem 27

The Bell rang loud and clear!
The little feet ran out with laughter and
chatter.
One more day has passed,
They ran fast, past the big gates.
Ran towards freedom and light!
The four walls had trapped them!
Inside was only the sound of their quiet
breathing.
They listened, their eyes looking out!
Looking out of that window;
Outside is freedom - waiting.
They waited with impatience
As the clock struck one,
Their little feet ran—ran fast
As Freedom and Light beckoned!

# Poem 28

Far away, the drums are beating
The quiet morning is filled with the rhythmic sound.
Beating—trying to evoke the force of the Goddess;
Little children with bare feet come running
The lush green of the field is filled with their laughter.
A lone woman quietly looks out -
Looks out of her window!
The childish prattle, the sound of the drums
Soothes her, filling her heart with a strange calm.

The Goddess will perhaps one day wipe out
the tears,
That for centuries have fallen—
Fallen from the eyes of Mothers, wives,
sisters, and daughters!